The Step-by-Step Way to Draw Turtle

A Fun and Easy Drawing Book to Learn How to Draw Turtles

By

Kristen Diaz.

License Notes

No part of this Book can be reproduced in any form or by any means including print, electronic, scanning or photocopying unless prior permission is granted by the author.

All ideas, suggestions and guidelines mentioned here are written for informative purposes. While the author has taken every possible step to ensure accuracy, all readers are advised to follow information at their own risk. The author cannot be held responsible for personal and/or commercial damages in case of misinterpreting and misunderstanding any part of this Book

Table of Contents

Introduction

Becoming a great artist requires creativity, patience and practice. These habits can flourish in children when they start to develop them at a young age. We believe our guide will teach your child the discipline and patience required to not just learn to draw well, but to use those qualities in everything they do. Your job as a parent is to work with your child and encourage them when stuck and feel like giving up.

The world of art is an amazing way for you and your child to communicate and bond. When you open this book and start to create with your little one, you will delight in the things you learn about them and they will feel closer to you. Your support and gentle suggestions will help them be more patient with themselves and soon they will take the time needed to create spectacular drawings of which you can both be proud.

This guide is useful for parents as it teaches fundamentals of drawing and simple techniques. By following this book with your child, adults will learn patience and develop their skills as a child's most important teacher. By spending a few hours together you will develop a strong connection and learn the best ways of communicating with each other. It is truly a rewarding experience when you and your child create a masterpiece by working together!

How to Draw Baby Turtle

STEP 1.

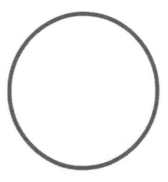

Draw a circle along the upper left part of the paper for the base of the head.

STEP 2.

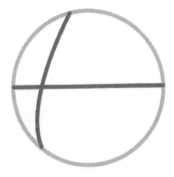

Divide the circle into sections with a horizontal line and a curve
vertical line.

STEP 3.

Trace the outline of the top part of the circle then draw a curve line along the right side of the circle shape like a question mark without the point at the end. Draw another curve line shape like diagonal letter "C" below the left bottom part of the circle for the outline of the nose. Draw a horizontal curve line under for the chin and a diagonal short line below the right end for the neck.

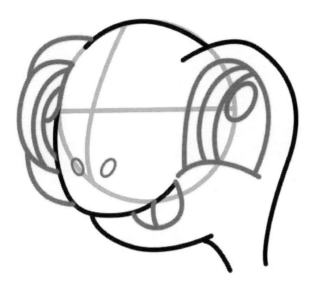

Draw the outline of the right eye shape like the upper half of a vertical oval with a horizontal curve line along the bottom. Draw parallel vertical line inside and a diagonal small oval for the pupil. Draw the outline of the left eye with parallel vertical curve line along the left side of the nose. Draw a curve line above and below the left eye for the outline of the left side of the head. Draw small diagonal ovals along the nose for the nostrils. Draw the outline of the mouth with a diagonal curve line below the right end of the nose shape like an inverted diagonal letter "C" with a small vertical curve line inside for the tongue.

STEP 5.

Draw the base of the shell shape like diagonal pointed end oval along the right side of the head.

STEP 6.

Draw the detail of the shell with a series of diagonal lines

forming a hexagon on the center.

STEP 7.

Draw a horizontal curve line below the bottom part of the shell for the bottom lining of the shell.

STEP 8.

Draw succeeding curve lines below the neck for the outline of the

bottom part of the body.

STEP 9.

Draw the outline of the right front leg shape like a curve top triangle with small curve lines along the bottom for the outline of the nails.

STEP 10.

Draw the outline of the left front leg with parallel curve line
going down and connected by a horizontal line at the end. Draw
small circles along the bottom for the nails.

STEP 11.

Draw the outline of the right back leg shape like a slim curve top triangle below the right bottom part of the shell. Draw a horizontal line connecting both right legs and passing behind the back right leg towards the shell for the outline of the bottom part of the body.

STEP 12.

Draw the outline of the left back leg between the right legs then draw small curve lines along the bottom for the nails.

Final outline. Erase all unnecessary base lines.

STEP 14.

You have to color it! Light green for the head, neck and legs. White, light blue and dark grey for the eyes. Dark grey for the nostrils. Red for the tongue. Green for the inside of the mouth and shell. Light brown for the bottom lining of the shell. Light yellow for the bottom part of the body and nails. That's it! Baby Turtle.

How to Draw Cartoon Sea Turtle

STEP 1.

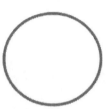

Draw a circle along the upper right part of the paper for the base
of the head.

STEP 2.

Draw the base of the upper lip with an angled curve line
overlapping the right upper half of the circle.

STEP 3.

Draw the outline of the eye with succeeding diagonal ovals. Draw

a curve line above the eye for the eyelid.

STEP 4.

Draw the outline of the head with curve line from the eyelid going diagonally down to the left and another one below the lower lip going diagonally down to the left. Draw small circles on both sides of the eye.

STEP 5.

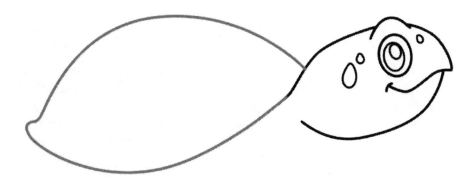

Draw the base of the shell shape like diagonal pointed end oval

from the head going down to the left.

STEP 6.

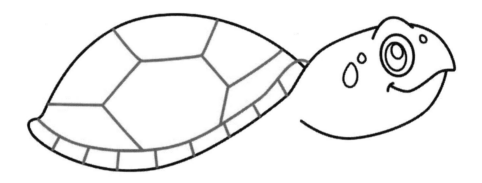

Draw a curve line parallel with the shell's bottom part then draw diagonal stripes along its length. Draw a series of diagonal lines for the details of the shell.

STEP 7.

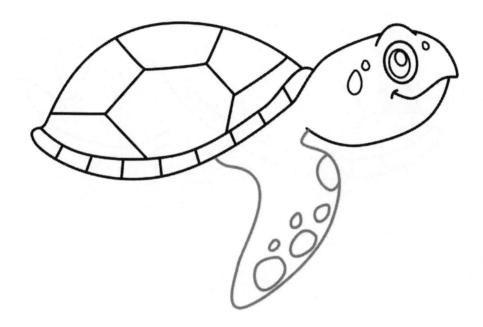

Draw the outline of the left front flipper with elongated curve line going down towards the left. Draw small circles inside for the details.

STEP 8.

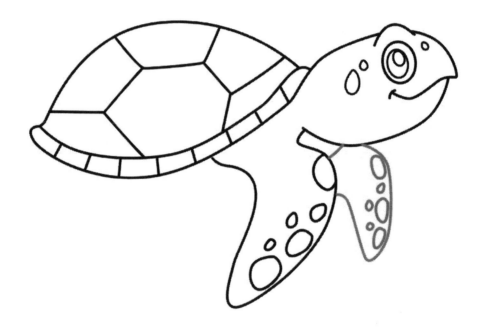

Draw the outline of the left front flipper with curve lines going below the head going down. Draw small vertical ovals and tiny circles inside for the details.

STEP 9.

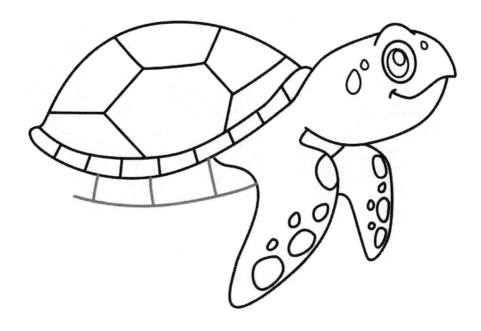

Draw the outline of the bottom part of the body with a horizontal curve
line below the shell and parallel diagonal stripes above.

STEP 10.

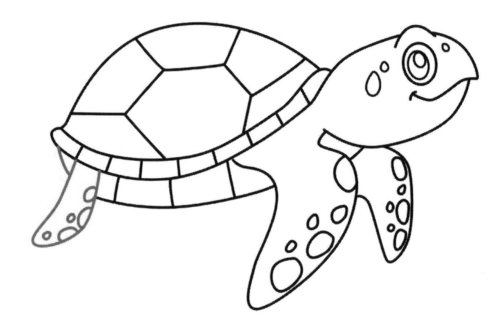

Draw the outline of the left back flipper with elongated curve line shape like diagonal letter "U" and a diagonal line along the top left side. Draw small curve lines and tiny circles inside for the details.

STEP 11.

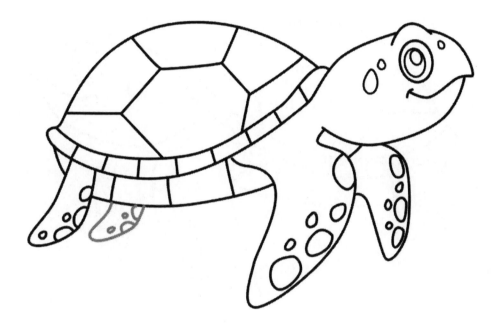

Draw the outline of the right back flipper below the bottom part of the body shape like diagonal letter "U". Draw small curve lines and tiny circles inside for the details.

STEP 12.

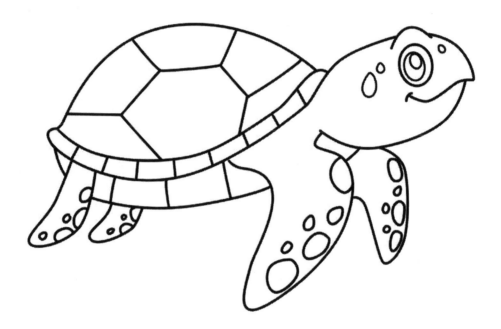

Final outline. Erase all unnecessary base lines.

STEP 13.

You have to color it! Green for the shell. Light green for the bottom lining of the shell and details of the face and flippers. Light yellow green for the head and flippers. Light yellow for the bottom part of the body. Black and white for the eye. That's it! Cartoon Sea Turtle.

How to Draw Cartoon Turtle

STEP 1.

Draw a horizontal oval along the left upper part of the paper for the base of the head.

Divide the oval into sections with a diagonal line and a curve
vertical line.

STEP 3.

Draw the base of the neck with parallel diagonal curve line from the head going down to the right.

Draw the outline of the eyes with a circle for the left eye and a diagonal oval for the right eye along the diagonal line dividing the head. Draw the outline of the pupils with succeeding vertical ovals inside each eye. Draw the outline of the mouth with a horizontal curve line and a deep curve line below with a diagonal curve line inside for the tongue.

STEP 5.

Trace the outline of the head and neck with a bulge above both eyes for the eyelids. Draw a small curve line above the eyelids for the eyebrows. Draw a small horizontal curve line below the mouth.

STEP 6.

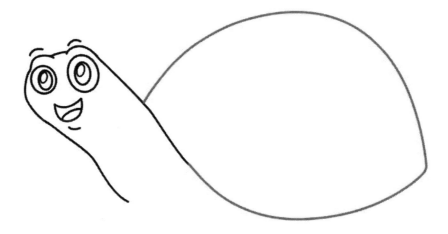

Draw the base of the shell with curve line from the right side of the neck going to the right.

STEP 7.

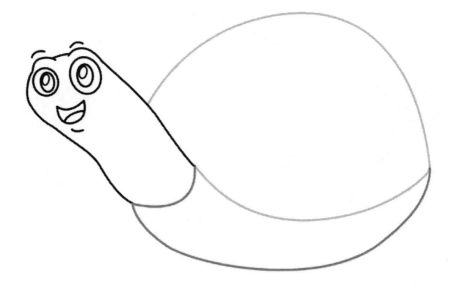

Draw a short curve line connecting both ends of the neck. Draw the base of the bottom part of the body with horizontal curve line.

STEP 8.

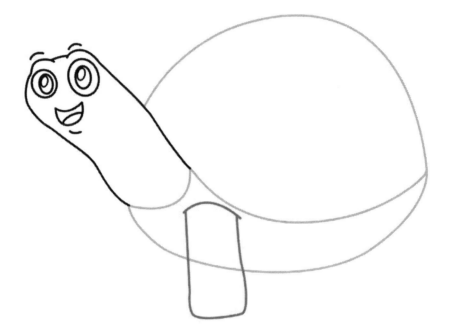

Draw the base of the right front leg shape like a tube going

diagonally down to the right.

STEP 9.

Draw the base of the left front leg below the neck going down.

STEP 10.

Draw the base of the right back leg shape like a diagonal curve

edge rectangle.

Draw the base of the left back leg shape like an open top square below the bottom part of the body.

STEP 12.

Trace the outline of the shell then draw a curve line parallel to the bottom lining then succeeding short curve lines below along its length. Draw a horizontal oval along the center of the shell and curve lines along the sides for the details.

STEP 13.

Trace the outline of the bottom part of the body. Draw diagonal stripes between the bottom part of the shell and body. Draw a small curve line for the outline of the tail shape like a diagonal letter "U".

STEP 14.

Trace the outline of the front legs. Draw small curve lines along
the bottom part of each leg for the nails.

STEP 15.

Trace the outline of the back legs. Draw small curve lines along the bottom part of the legs for the outline of the nails.

STEP 16.

Final outline. Erase all unnecessary base lines.

STEP 17.

You have to color it! Desaturated green for the shell. Yellow for the details of the shell and nails. Light brown for the linings of the shell. Light green for the head, neck, tail and legs. Black and white for the eyes. Desaturated dark green for the inside of the mouth. Red for the tongue. Desaturated yellow for the bottom part of the body. That's it! Cartoon Turtle.

How to Draw Cute Turtle

STEP 1.

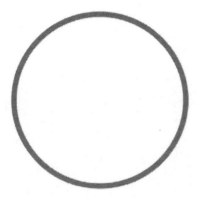

Draw a circle along the upper left part of the paper for the base of
the head.

STEP 2.

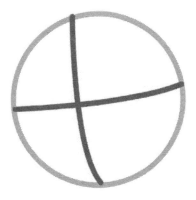

Divide the circle into sections with a curve vertical and diagonal
line.

STEP 3.

Draw the outline of the eyes with small circles along the diagonal line dividing the head with diagonal small oval inside each for the pupils. Draw the outline of the lips shape like letter "U".

STEP 4.

Draw the outline of the head by tracing the upper part of the circle with curve line going down towards the right.

STEP 5.

Draw the base of the shell with a pointed end curve line from the right side of the head going towards the right.

STEP 6.

Draw a horizontal curve line parallel to the bottom part of the shell.

STEP 7.

Draw the details of the shell with a diagonal oval on the center part and curve lines along the side.

STEP 8.

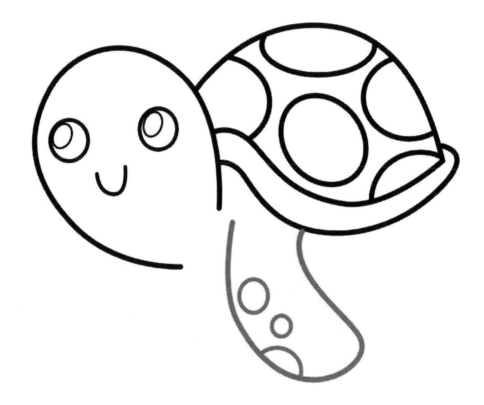

Draw the outline of the right front flipper shape like an elongated curve letter "U" with small circles and small curve line inside for the details.

STEP 9.

Draw the outline of the left flipper shape like a diagonal letter "U" with small circles inside for the details. Draw a horizontal slim letter "U" beside the right top part of the flipper connecting it towards the right front flipper.

STEP 10.

Draw the outline of the bottom part of the body with a diagonal curve line from the right front flipper going diagonally up towards the right bottom part of the shell. Draw the outline of the right back flipper shape like diagonal curve letter "U" below the right bottom part of the shell with small circles inside for the details. Draw the outline of the left back flipper with small curve line shape like diagonal letter "U" between the right front and back leg then draw small circles inside for the details.

Final outline. Erase all unnecessary base lines.

STEP 12.

You have to color it! Green for the head and flippers. Light green for the shell and details of the flippers. Desaturated light green for the details of the shell. Desaturated yellow for the lining of the shell and bottom part of the body. Black and white for the eyes. That's it! Cute Turtle.

How to Draw Simple Cartoon Turtle

STEP 1.

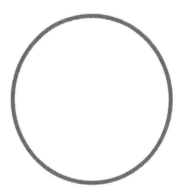

Draw a circle along the upper right part of the paper for the base

of the head.

STEP 2.

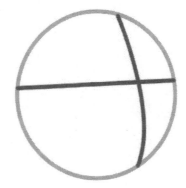

Divide the circle into sections with a horizontal line and a curve vertical line.

STEP 3.

Draw the outline of the lower part of the head and neck with a diagonal slightly curve vertical line along the left side and a curve line along the right curving diagonally down to the left.

STEP 4.

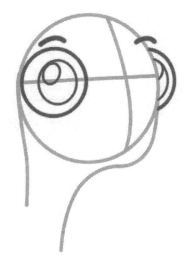

Draw the outline of the left eye with succeeding circle and a diagonal small oval inside for the pupil. Draw the outline of the right eye with succeeding vertical curve line along the right outer side of the head and a small diagonal curve line inside for the pupil. Draw a short horizontal curve line above both eyes for the eyebrows.

STEP 5.

Draw the outline of the mouth shape like a diagonal crescent moon with a curve line inside for the tongue. Draw a diagonal short curve line below the mouth.

STEP 6.

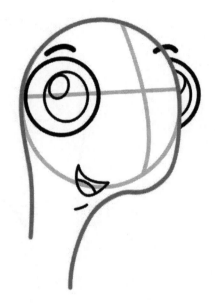

Trace the outline of the head.

Draw the base of the body with diagonal curve lines from the
neck going down and a circle at the end.

STEP 8.

Draw the base of the right arm with parallel curve line from the right upper side of the body going up to the right and the base of the hand at the end showing four fingers pointing up. Draw a small circle for the elbow.

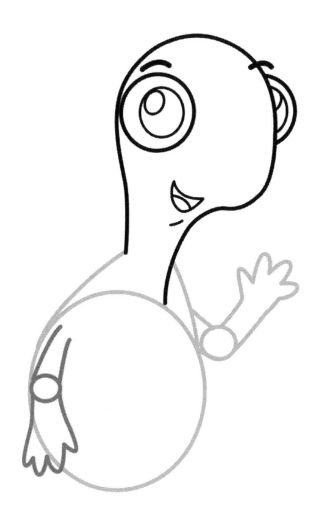

Draw the base of the left arm with parallel vertical curve line along the left part of the base of the body going down and the base of the hand at the end showing four fingers pointing down. Draw a small circle for the elbow.

STEP 10.

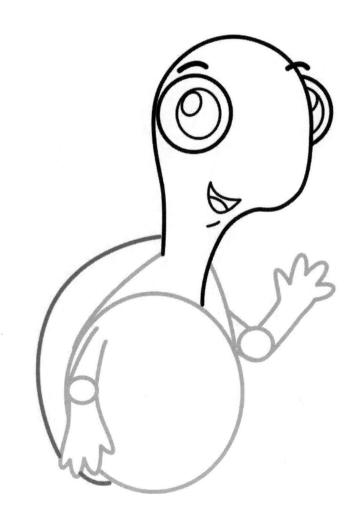

Draw the base of the shell with a curve line from the left side of the neck going down below the left hand.

STEP 11.

Draw the base of the left leg shape like elongated open top
vertical triangle with a small curve line on top.

Draw the base of the right leg shape like an open top elongated vertical triangle.

Trace the outline of the right and bottom part of the body. Draw a curve line across the bottom part of the neck for the collar.

Trace the outline of the right arm and hand then draw a small

diagonal curve line across the palm.

STEP 15.

Trace the outline of the left arm and hand. Draw a curve line
enclosing the top part of the arm for the sleeve.

Trace the outline of the shell then draw small curve lines for the bottom lining of the shell. Draw horizontal curve stripes along the front body.

STEP 17.

Trace the outline of the legs then draw small curve lines along the bottom part of each leg for the nails. Draw a short diagonal line along the center part of each leg.

Final outline. Erase all unnecessary base lines.

STEP 19.

You have to color it! Light green for the head, neck, arms, hands and legs. Black and white for the eyes. Desaturated green for the inside of the mouth and shell. Red for the tongue. Desaturated yellow green for the bottom lining of the shell. Desaturated yellow for the front body. Yellow for the nails. That's it! Simple Cartoon Turtle.

How to Draw Turtle with Okay Sign

STEP 1.

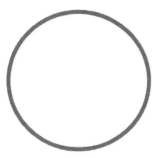

Draw a circle along the upper part of the paper for the base of the head.

STEP 2.

Divide the circle into sections with a diagonal line and a curve

vertical line.

STEP 3.

Draw the outline of the right eye shape like the upper half of a vertical oval with a horizontal curve line at the end. Draw the outline of the left eye shape like the upper half of a vertical oval with a longer curve line along the inner side of the eye and a horizontal curve line along the bottom. Draw the outline of the pupils with vertical curve line inside each eye. Draw a curve line above both eyes for the eyelids.

STEP 4.

Trace the outline of the top part of the head then draw both sides of the head with vertical curve line from both parts of the eyebrows going down. Draw the outline of the bottom part of the nose with horizontal curve line and a small diagonal curve line below the right end of the nose for the mouth. Draw a small vertical curve line inside the mouth for the outline of the tongue. Draw a small horizontal curve line below the mouth.

Draw the base of the body with parallel diagonal curve lines from both sides of the neck going down and a circle at the end.

Draw the base of the right arm from the right upper part of the base of the body curving down and the base of the hand at the end showing four fingers clenched into fist. Draw a small circle for the elbow.

STEP 7.

Draw the outline of the left arm with parallel diagonal line going down towards the left and the base of the hand at the end showing three fingers clenched into fist and the thumb pointing upward. Draw a small circle for the elbow.

STEP 8.

Draw the base of the shell with a curve line shape like inverted

diagonal letter "C".

STEP 9.

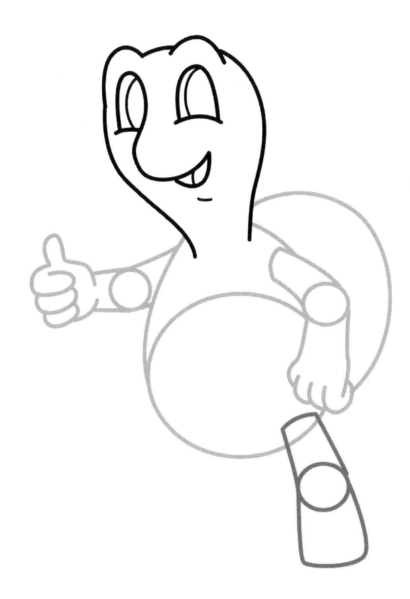

Draw the base of the right leg from the right bottom part of the base of the body going diagonally down to the right. Draw a circle for the knee.

Draw the base of the left leg with parallel horizontal line going diagonally down to the left and connected by a horizontal line at the end. Draw a circle for the knee.

STEP 11.

Trace the outline of the right arm and hand. Draw a vertical
curve line enclosing the top part of the arm.

STEP 12.

Trace the outline of the body and shell. Draw a curve line enclosing the bottom part of the neck. Draw horizontal curve stripes along the length of the body. Draw a diagonal curve line from the right side of the neck going down the outer side of the right arm for the outline of the bottom lining of the shell. Draw small diagonal lines along the length of the lining. Draw a series of diagonal lines for the details of the shell.

STEP 13.

Trace the outline of the left arm and hand.

STEP 14.

Trace the outline of the right leg then draw small curve lines
along the bottom part of the leg for the nails.

Trace the outline of the left leg then draw small curve lines along the bottom part of the leg for the outline of the nails.

Final outline. Erase all unnecessary base lines.

STEP 17.

You have to color it! Light green for the head, neck, arms, hands and legs. Black and white for the eyes. Green for the inside of the mouth and shell. Red for the tongue. Yellow for the body and nails. Light brown for the linings of the shell. That's it! Turtle with Okay Sign.

How to Draw Turtle Riding A Skateboard

STEP 1.

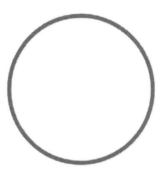

Draw a circle along the upper part of the paper for the base of the head.

STEP 2.

Divide the circle into sections with a curve vertical and horizontal line.

STEP 3.

Draw the outline of the right eye with a vertical oval and succeeding circles inside for the outline of the pupil. Draw the outline of the nose with a vertical curve line along the lower left part of the circle. Draw the outline of the left eye with a curve line along the left upper side of the nose. Draw the outline of the pupil with succeeding curve lines inside.

STEP 4.

Draw the outline of the cap shape like an inverted bowl overlapping the upper part of the circle. Draw an open bottom part rectangle above the front bottom part of the cap with a horizontal line below and a short vertical line along the bottom. Draw the detail of the top part of the cap shape like the upper half of a small vertical oval with a short diagonal curve line below going down towards the rectangle. Draw the outline of the cap's brim with a curve line shape like a horizontal letter "U" along the right lower side of the cap.

Draw the outline of both sides of the head with vertical curve lines from both bottom end of the cap going down as shown above. Draw the outline of the mouth with diagonal curve line and a deep diagonal shorter curve line below. Draw the outline of the tongue with a diagonal curve line inside.

STEP 6.

Draw the base of the body with parallel diagonal curve lines from the bottom part of the neck going down towards the left and a circle at the end.

STEP 7.

Draw the base of the right arm with parallel curve line from the upper right side of the body curving down to the right and the base of the hand at the end clenched into fist. Draw a small circle for the elbow.

STEP 8.

Draw the base of the left arm with parallel diagonal line going down to the left and the base of the hand at the end showing four fingers. Draw a small circle for the elbow.

STEP 9.

Draw the base of the shell with a curve line from the left cheek going down towards the left bottom part of the base of the body passing behind the left arm.

STEP 10.

Draw the base of the left leg from the lower left part of the base of the body curving down to the left. Draw a small circle for the knee.

STEP 11.

Draw the base of the right leg with curve line from the right lower side of the base of the body going down. The leg appears to be bended upward. Draw a small circle for the knee.

STEP 12.

Draw the outline of a skateboard shape like an elongated diagonal oval enclosing the bottom part of both legs. Draw the outline of the wheel below the board as shown above.

Trace the outline of the right arm and hand.

STEP 14.

Trace the outline of the left arm and hand.

Trace the outline of the body then draw curve horizontal stripes inside. Draw a vertical curve line parallel to the outline of the left side of the body for the bottom lining of the shell. Draw short diagonal stripes along its length.

STEP 16.

Trace the outline of the outer part of the shell. Draw a diagonal
line shape like letter Y" above the arm and an inverted letter "Y"
below the arm for the details of the shell.

STEP 17.

Trace the outline of both legs then draw small curve lines along the bottom part of each leg for the outline of the nails.

Trace the outline of the skateboard then draw a small circle

inside each wheel.

Final outline. Erase all unnecessary base lines.

STEP 20.

You have to color it! Light blue for the hat. Light green for the head, neck, arms, hands and legs. White for the eyes. Light green and black for the pupils. Green for the inside of the mouth and shell. Red for the tongue. Light brown for the linings of the shell. Yellow for the body and nails. Desaturated light blue for the board. Grey and white for the wheels. That's it! Turtle Riding Skateboard.

About the Author

Kristen Diaz is an accomplished artist and e-book author living in Southern California. She has provided the illustrations for hundreds of children's books as her realistic and lifelike images appeal to children and adults alike.

Diaz began her career as an artist when she was in her 20's creating caricatures on the beaches of sunny California. What started as a way to make extra spending money turned into a successful career because of her amazing talent. Her comically accurate caricatures had a unique look and one of the local authors took notice. When the writer asked Diaz to illustrate one of her books, Kristen jumped at the opportunity to showcase her talent. The result was spectacular and soon Diaz was in high demand. Her ability to change her style to fit the books made her an attractive artist to work with.

She decided to get a more formal education in graphic design and illustration by enrolling in the Arts program at Platt's College which is where she met the love of her life and life partner, Terri. The two live in Pasadena close to the beach where Diaz' career first flourished. She occasionally hangs out on the beach with her easel and paints and makes caricatures of the humanity passing by. Her e-books are simple to follow and contain many witty anecdotes about her life in Pasadena.

Made in the USA
Coppell, TX
14 November 2021